HAVE FUN AND ENJOY OUR SEX COUPONS!

DON'T FORGET TO FILL OUT THE COUPONS THAT WE LEFT BLANK FOR YOU!

- STEAMY SARAH

NAUGHTY NAUGHTY

EROTIC MASSAGE

NAUGHTY NAUGHTY

ORAL SEX WITH MINTS

NAUGHTY NAUGHTY

NAKED LAP DANCE SEX

NAUGHTY NAUGHTY

KITCHEN COUNTER SEX

NAUGHTY NAUGHTY

SHOWER SEX

NAUGHTY NAUGHTY

MUTUAL
MASTURBATION

NAUGHTY NAUGHTY

ORAL SEX
UNTIL ORGASM

NAUGHTY NAUGHTY

30 MINUTES
OF EDGING

NAUGHTY NAUGHTY

LIVING ROOM SEX

NAUGHTY NAUGHTY

2 MINUTE QUICKIE

NAUGHTY NAUGHTY

SEX STANDING UP

NAUGHTY NAUGHTY

ORAL SEX WITH ICE

NAUGHTY NAUGHTY

ORAL SEX
WITH BLINDFOLDS

NAUGHTY NAUGHTY

SILENT SEX

NAUGHTY NAUGHTY

WAKE PARTNER UP
WITH ORAL SEX

NAUGHTY NAUGHTY

ROLE PLAY SEX

NAUGHTY NAUGHTY

SEX WITH HANDCUFFS

NAUGHTY NAUGHTY

DRUNK SEX

NAUGHTY NAUGHTY

ANAL SEX

NAUGHTY NAUGHTY

ORAL SEX
FROM THE BACK

NAUGHTY NAUGHTY

MAKE PARTNER ORGASM WITH LUBE

NAUGHTY NAUGHTY

MAKE PARTNER
ORGASM WITH LOTION

NAUGHTY NAUGHTY

MAKE PARTNER
ORGASM WITH HANDS

NAUGHTY NAUGHTY

MAKE PARTNER
ORGASM WITH TONGUE

NAUGHTY NAUGHTY

MAKE PARTNER
ORGASM WITH LIPS

NAUGHTY NAUGHTY

ORAL SEX WITH
WHIPPED CREAM

NAUGHTY NAUGHTY

SEX RIGHT AFTER A WORKOUT

NAUGHTY NAUGHTY

1 HOUR OF EDGING

NAUGHTY NAUGHTY

DRY HUMP SEX

NAUGHTY NAUGHTY

ORGASM IN
PARTNER'S MOUTH

NAUGHTY NAUGHTY

NAUGHTY NAUGHTY

NAUGHTY NAUGHTY

NAUGHTY NAUGHTY

NAUGHTY NAUGHTY

NAUGHTY NAUGHTY

NAUGHTY NAUGHTY

NAUGHTY NAUGHTY

NAUGHTY NAUGHTY

NAUGHTY NAUGHTY

NAUGHTY NAUGHTY

NAUGHTY NAUGHTY

NAUGHTY NAUGHTY

NAUGHTY NAUGHTY

NAUGHTY NAUGHTY

NAUGHTY NAUGHTY

NAUGHTY NAUGHTY

NAUGHTY NAUGHTY

NAUGHTY NAUGHTY

NAUGHTY NAUGHTY

NAUGHTY NAUGHTY

Made in the USA
Las Vegas, NV
07 December 2024

13481118R00057